Ten Songs from
Des Knaben Wunderhorn
in Full Score

The composer's original scoring for solo voice with orchestra
Texts in German and English

GUSTAV MAHLER

DOVER PUBLICATIONS, INC.
Mineola, New York

Mahler's orchestral settings of three additional texts
from *Des Knaben Wunderhorn* are available
in the following Dover editions:

For "Urlicht":
Symphonies Nos. 1 and 2 in Full Score
(Dover 0-486-25473-9)

For "Es sungen drei Engel" and "Das himmlische Leben":
Symphonies Nos. 3 and 4 in Full Score
(Dover 0-486-26166-2)

———————

Including text only of "Das himmlische Leben,"
all 24 of Mahler's *Wunderhorn* settings are available in:

Des Knaben Wunderhorn and the Rückert Lieder for Voice and Piano
(Dover 0-486-40634-2)

Bibliographical Note

This Dover edition, first published in 2001, is a one-volume compilation of *Des Knaben Wunderhorn / Lieder für eine Singstimme mit Orchesterbegleitung von Gustav Mahler,* originally published in two volumes by Universal-Edition, Vienna, n.d. [1905]. The prefatory note and lists of contents and instrumentation are newly added. Portions of the note on page iii were freely adapted from Donald Mitchell's Mahler entry in Volume 11 of *The New Grove Dictionary of Music and Musicians* (© Macmillan Publishers Limited, London 1980).

We are indebted to composer David L. Post for bringing these works to our attention, and to the Amos Music Library, Miami University (Ohio), for providing the scores for republication.

International Standard Book Number: 0-486-41693-3

Manufactured in the United States of America
Dover Publications, Inc., 31 East 2nd Street, Mineola, N.Y. 11501

NOTE

Published in 1806 and 1808, *Des Knaben Wunderhorn* (The Youth's Miraculous Horn) was a gathering of folksongs and folksong-style poems collected, retouched, or made up out of whole cloth by poets Achim von Arnim and Clemens Brentano to reflect their concept of German folk poetry. In 1887, Gustav Mahler discovered the musical potential of this collection, providing him with most of his song texts over the next fourteen years.

Applying his personal experiences to reinterpret literary thought (something he did all his life through composition), Mahler created musical settings that elevated poetry beyond the realm of medieval fairy tale, transforming poetic images into symbols of his own vision of Man's (or the Artist's) experience of the world. In this way, Mahler's *Wunderhorn* pieces function as a self-focused storehouse of invention, symbol and image akin to the symphonic music he wrote in those same years and later.

Barely into his thirties, Mahler's extraordinarily fertile period of 1892–96 saw a burst of *Wunderhorn* activity in the form of the ten "Songs for a Solo Voice with Orchestral Accompaniment"—the present collection— and of his first four symphonies. While the autobiographical First Symphony ("Titan") quotes themes from Mahler's *Songs of a Wayfarer* but has no *sung* text, the three symphonies that follow continued the composer's intensely personalized *Wunderhorn* activity, incorporating vocal settings of "Urlicht" (Primordial Light) in No. 2; of "Es sungen drei Engel" (Three Angels Were Singing) in No. 3; and of "Das himmlische Leben" (Heavenly Life) in No. 4.

In 1905, Universal-Edition published the ten orchestral song settings as a group, in two volumes, providing an edition that combined the German text underlay, an English singing translation by Addie Funk, and performance indications (tempi and the like) in both German and Italian.

The same songs are included in *Des Knaben Wunderhorn and the Rückert Lieder for Voice and Piano,* a 1999 Dover compilation that includes all twenty-four *Wunderhorn* songs drawn from early publications by Universal-Edition, B. Schott's Söhne, and C. F. Kahnt. (Only "Das himmlische Leben" is represented by text alone.) Students of these works have indicated that there are differences— some significant—between the versions for voice and piano and the present scores for voice and orchestra, reflecting Mahler's thinking at the time.

CONTENTS

Der Schildwache Nachtlied 1
The sentinel's nightsong

Verlorne Müh' 28
Labor lost

Trost im Unglück 42
Solace in sorrow

Wer hat dies Liedel erdacht? 63
. . . Up there on the hill . . .

Das irdische Leben 74
Earthly life

Des Antonius von Padua Fischpredigt 100
Antonius of Padua's fish sermon

Rheinlegendchen 125
Little legend of the Rhine

Lied des Verfolgten im Turm 138
Song of the persecuted man in the tower

Wo die schönen Trompeten blasen 172
Where the beautiful trumpets blow

Lob des hohen Verstands 185
In praise of lofty intelligence

INSTRUMENTATION

Mahler's scoring varies from song to song, selecting instruments from the following list.

Piccolo [Flauto piccolo, Fl. picc.]
2 Flutes [Flauti, Fl.]
2 Oboes [Oboi, Ob.]
English Horn [Corno inglese, Cor. ingl.]
2 Clarinets in A, B♭ [Clarinetti, Cl. (La, Si♭)]
E♭ Clarinet [Clarinetto, Cl. (Mi♭)]
3 Bassoons [Fagotti, Fg.]

4 Horns in F [Corni, Cor. (Fa)]
 2 Trumpets in F, B♭ [Trombe, Tr. (Fa, Si♭)]
Trombone [Trombone, Trb.]
Tuba [Tuba, Tb.]

Timpani [Timpani, Timp.]

Percussion
    Bass Drum [Gran Cassa, Gr. C.]
    Cymbals [Piatti, Ptti.]
    Rute*
    Snare Drum [Tamburo militaire, Tamb. mil., Tbr. mil.]
    Tam-tam [Tamtam, Tamt.]
    Triangle [Triangolo, Trgl.]

Harp [Arpa, Arp.]

Solo Voice [Voce]

Violins I, II [Violino, Vl.]
Viola [Viola, Vla.]
Cello [Violoncello, Vlc.]
Bass [Contrabasso, Cb.]

---

*"The Germans had, or have, a sort of birch-broom, called *Ruthe,* with which to beat the bass drum. The player is evidently meant to beat 8ths with the *Ruthe* and quarters with the ordinary bass-drum stick. Mahler has revived this method . . ."

(Forsyth, *Orchestration*)

Ten Songs from
Des Knaben Wunderhorn

Der Schildwache Nachtlied

The sentinel's nightsong

English version by
Addie Funk

1

Wenn al - le Leu - te schla - - fen,
When oth - ers rest are tak - - ing,

Fl.
Ob.
Cor. ingl.
Cl.
Fg.
Cor.
Tr.
Tbr. mil.
Ptti.
Voce
so muß ich wa - chen! Ja wa - chen!
I must be wak - ing, yes wak - ing!
Vl. I
Vl. II
Vla.
Vlc.
Cb.
pizz.

rit.
Fl. picc.
Fl.
Ob.
Cor. ingl.
Cl.
Fg.
Cor.
Tr.
aperto
Trgl.
Tbr. mil.
Ptti.
Gr.C.
Arp.
Voce
Muß trau - rig sein!
Must mourn - ful be!
Vl.I
Vl.II
Vla.
Vlc.
Cb.
pizz.
arco
div.

Etwas langsamer
Un poco più lento
veloce
15
Cor. ingl.
veloce
1.
p
Cl.
Arp.
Voce
Lieb'
Ah,
Etwas langsamer
sempre con sord.
Vl.I
Vl.II
Vla.
con sord.
arco
pp
Vlc.
Cb.
15

Kna-be, du mußt nicht trau-rig sein! Will dei-ner warten im Rosen -
sweetheart, thou must not mournful be. Will wait thy coming 'mid ro-ses

gar-ten, im grü - nen Klee, im grü - nen
blooming in verd - ant mead! in verd - ant

Anmerkung für den Dirigenten: Die kleinen Holzbläserfiguren werden ohne Rücksicht auf das allgemeine *Ritenuto* schneller, nämlich entsprechend dem früheren Tempo ausgeführt.

Nota per il direttore d'orchestra: *Le piccole figure segnate ai legni si facciano eseguire sempre in tempo, leggere e veloci, senza alcun riguardo in rapporto al tempo ritenuto conforme alla canzone.*

Note to the conductor: Regardless of the general *ritenuto,* the small figures given to the woodwinds should be played quicker i. e. in a tempo corresponding to the former one.

Tempo I

Fl.
Ob.
Cor. ingl.
Cl.
Fg.
Cor.
Timp.
Tbr. mil.
Gr.C.
Voce

Zum grünen Klee
To verdant mead
da geh' ich nicht!
I can-not come!

Tempo I

Vl.I
Vl.II
Vla.
Vlc.
Cb.

Etwas gemessener
35
Un poco più moderato
Fl.
Ob.
Cor. ingl.
Cl.
Fg.
Verzierungen sehr schnell
Gruppetti molto presto
Cor.
Tr.
Tbr. mil.
Gr.C.
Voce
Zum Waf-fen - gar - ten
Have tryst full bit - - ter!
Voll Hel-le -
Where hal-berds
Etwas gemessener
Vl.I
Vl.II
Vla.
Vlc.
Cb.
pizz.
35

Fl. picc.
Fl.
Ob.
Cor. ingl.
Cl.
Fg.
Cor.
Tr.
Timp.
Trgl.
Tamb. mil.
Ptti.
Gr. C.
Voce
Vl. I
Vl. II
Vla.
Vlc.
Cb.
sempre p
a2
etwas hervortretend
poco rilevato
(Becken an der gr. Tr. befestigt)
(fermare i piatti sulla cassa)
par- - - - ten
glit- - - - ter!
bin ich ge-
There is my
pizz.
arco

Poco rit.
40
Fl. picc.
Fl.
a 2
verklingend
spegnendosi
Ob.
a 2
verkling.
spegnend.
Cor. ingl.
Cl.
Fg.
Cor.
Tr.
Timp.
Trgl.
Tamb. mil.
Ptti.
Gr. C.
verklingend
spegnendosi
Voce
stellt!
post!
Bin ich ge-stellt!
There is my post!
arco
pizz.
Poco rit.
Vl. I
Vl. II
arco
div.
dim.
Vla.
Vlc.
Cb.
40

verklingend
spegnendosi
45
Langsamer
Più lento
Fl.
Ob.
Cl.
Cor.
Tr.
Timp.
Arp.
poco rit.
Voce
Stehst
Art
Langsamer
immer noch mit Dämpfer
arco
veloce
Vl. I
Vl. II
sempre ancora con sord.
Vla.
immer noch mit Dämpfer
pizz.
Vlc.
con sord.
arco
Cb.

50
Fl.
1.
Cl.
veloce
1.
p
Fg.
1.
pp
Cor.
4.
pp
Arp.
Voce
du im Feld, so helf' dir Gott! An Got-tes Se-gen ist alles ge -
with the host, then help thee God! To have His blessing is all pos -
Vl. I
Vl. II
Vla.
arco
pp
Vlc.
div.
Cb.
50

55
Fl.
a 2
pp
Cor. ingl.
pp
Cl.
1.
Fg.
1.
p
Cor.
4.
p
Arp.
Voce
le-gen! Wer's glau - ben tut! Wer's glauben tut!
sessing, who so be - lieves, who so be - - lieves!
espress.
Vl. I
pp
Vl. II
Vla.
Vlc.
55

rit.
Tempo I
Fl.
a 2
60
Ob.
1.
Cor. ingl.
Cl.
prit.
Fg.
Cor.
4.
Timp.
Arp.
Voce
Wer's glauben tut,
Who so_be-lieves,
Vl. I
div.
sich gänzlich verlierend
senza sord.
Vl. II
perdendosi dell tutto
Vla.
sich gänzlich verlierend
Vlc.
senza sord
pizz.
arco
perdendosi dell tutto
Cb.
senza sord.
60

Etwas gemessener
Un poco più moderato
65
Fl. picc.
Fl.
Ob.
Cor. ingl.
Cl.
Fg.
Cor.
Timp.
Trgl.
Tamb. mil.
Ptti.
Gr. C.
Voce
Vl. I
Vl. II
Vla.
Vlc.
Cb.
a 2
Die Vorschläge sehr schnell auszuführen – l'appogiature eseguire molto presto
Oberstimme etwas hervortretend
mf rilevare la voce superiore
Becken frei, mit Schwammschlägel
Piatti liberi, con bacchette di spugna
ist weit davon!
is far a-way!
Etwas gemessener
pizz.
65

ohne Nachschlag
senza aggiunzione
a 2
Cl.
Fg.
Cor.
con sord.
Tr.
Tamb. mil.
Voce
Er ist ein Kö - nig! Er ist ein
He is a rul - - - er! he is an
Vl. I
Vl. II
ohne Nachschlag
senza aggiunzione
Vla.
Vlc.
Cb.

ohne Nachschlag
senza aggiunzione
70
Fl.
Ob.
Cor. ingl.
Cl.
Fg.
Cor.
Timp.
Trgl.
Tamb. mil.
Voce
a 2
ppp
pp
p
mf
f
Kai - - ser! Ein Kai - ser!
Er führt den
emp' - - ror, an emp' - ror!
He wa - ges
Vl. I
Vl. II
Vla.
Vlc.
Cb.
pizz.
arco
tr
70

75
Fl. picc.
Fl.
Ob.
Cor. ingl.
Cl.
Fg.
Cor.
Tr.
Timp.
Trgl.
Tamb. mil.
Becken frei, mit Schwammschlägel
Piatti liberi, con bacchette di spugna
Ptti.
Den Ruf der Schildwachen nachahmen
Imitando il comando della sentinella
offener Ton
suono aperto
Voce
Krieg!
war!
Halt!
Halt!
Wer da!!
Who goes
Vl. I
Vl. II
ohne Nachschlag
senza aggiunzione
Vla.
Vlc.
Cb.
75

poco a poco cresc. al
ohne Nachschlag
(senza aggiunzione)
a 2
Fl.
Ob.
Cl.
Fg.
Cor.
Tr.
Timp.
Trgl.
Tbr. mil.
Ptti.
cresc. al
Voce
there?
Rund'!
Th'round!
arco
ohne Nachschlag - senza aggiunzione
Vl. I
Vl. II
pizz.
Vla.
Vlc.
Cb.

poco a poco dim.
80
Fl. picc.
Fl.
Ob.
Cor. ingl.
Cl.
Fg.
Cor.
Tr.
Timp.
Trgl.
Thr. mil.
Ptti.
Voce
a 2
tr
mit Teller - col piatto
poco a poco dim.
Vl. I
Vl. II
Vla.
Vlc.
Cb.
arco
80

Fl.
Ob.
Cor. ingl.
Cl.
Fg.
Cor.
Tr.
Timp.
Trgl.
Tbr. mil.
Ptti.
Voce
Vl.I
Vl.II
Vla.
Vlc.
Cb.
85
a 2
(Oberstimme gut hervortreten)
(bene rilevare la voce superiore)
pizz.
arco

Fl. picc.
Fl.
Ob.
Cor. ingl.
Cl.
Fg.
Cor.
Tr.
Timp.
Trgl.
Tbr. mil.
Ptti.
Gr. C.
Arp.
Voce
Vl. I
Vl. II
Vla.
Vlc.
Cb.
(sich verlierend)
(perdendosi)
dim.
pizz.
arco
div.
Bleib' mir vom Leib!
Stand off from me!

90
rit.
Lento (♩♩♩ = ♩♩♩)
Fl. picc.
Fl.
Ob.
Cor. ingl.
Cl.
Tr.
Timp.
Trgl.
Tbr. mil.
Arp.
Voce
1.
(verklingend)
(spegnendosi)
Wer
Who
rit.
(4 fach get.)
(div. in 4)
con sord.
unis.
espr.
Vl. I
Vl. II
arco
pizz.
Vla.
Vlc.
Cb.
90

95
Fl.
Ob.
Cor. ingl.
Cl.
Cor.
Arp.
Voce
Vl. S.
Vl. I
Vl. II
Vla.
Vlc.
zart tenero
arco
p espr.
sangeshier? Wer sangzurStund?
sang it here? Whence came the sound?
Ver-lor - ne Feld - wacht
Ill-fat - ed sen - ti - nel
95

1.
100
Fl.
pp
Ob.
fp
ppp
Cor ingl.
Cl.
Cor.
4.
Timp.
Arp.
f
p
deutlich
distinto
Voce
sang es um Mit - - ter - nacht! Mit - ter-nacht!
chant-ed his mid - - night knell! Mid - night knell!
Vl. S.
Vl. I
Vl. II
Vla.
Vlc.
Cb.
pizz.

molto rit.
105
Fl.
Ob.
Cor. ingl.
Cl.
Cor.
Timp.
Arp.
Voce
Vl. I Solo
Vl. II Solo
Vl. I
Vl. II
Vla.
Vlc.
Cb.
bis zur gänzlichen Unhörbarkeit
fino che si spegni del tutto
Mit-ter-nacht!
Midnight knell!
deutlich-distinto
Feld - wacht!
Sen - ti - nel!
pizz.
arco
Solo
bis zur gänzlichen Unhörbarkeit abnehmen
dim. fino che si spegni del tutto
105

Verlorne Müh'

Labor lost

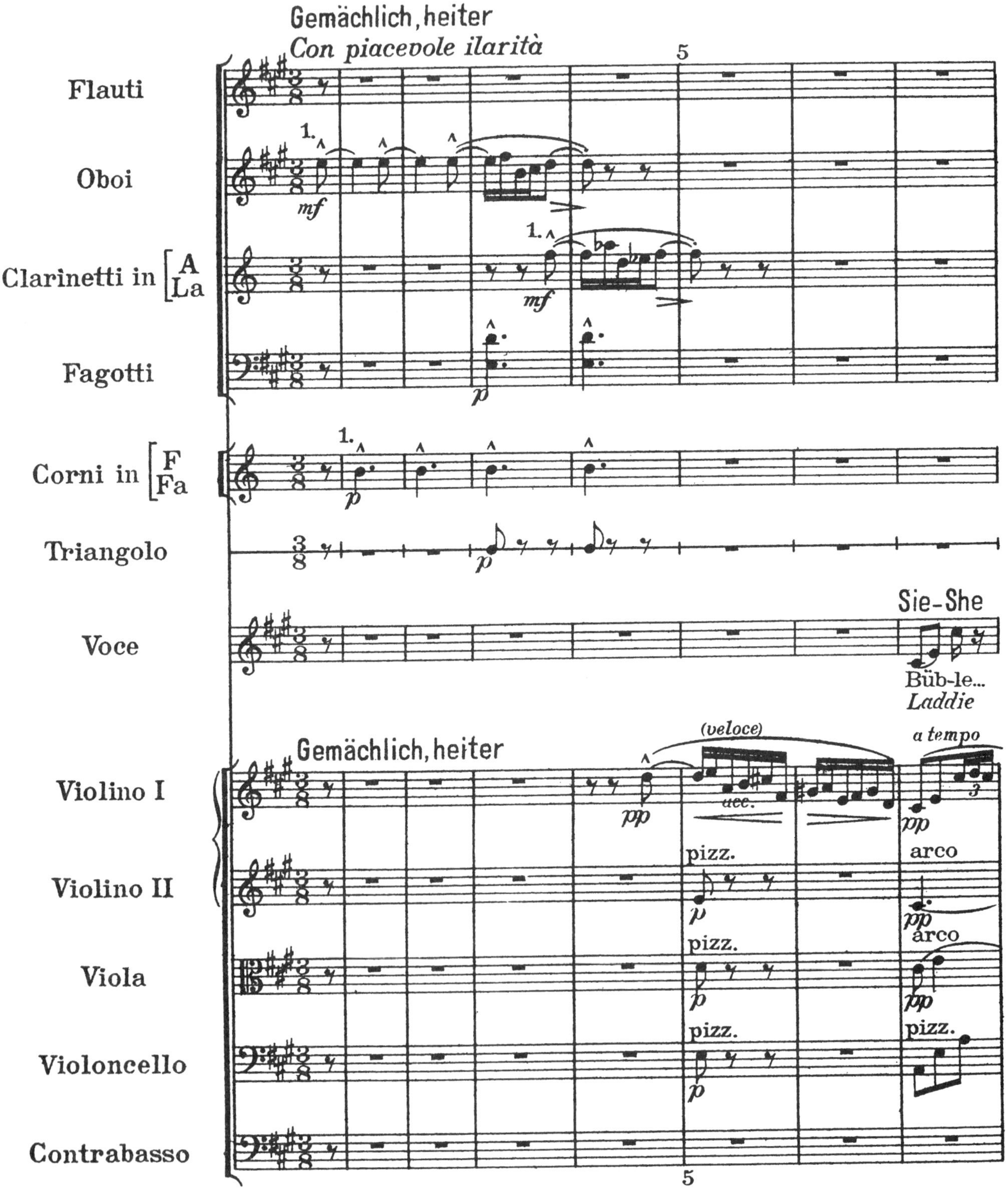

10
Etwas zurückhaltend
a 2
Fl.
1.
Ob.
Cl.
2.
Fg.
Cor.
Zeit lassen
Non affrettarsi
Voce
wir!
dear.
Büb-le, wir wollen aus-se-ge-he! aus-se-ge-he!
Laddie, you will go out with me, out with me!
Poco ritard.
pizz.
arco
Vl. I
Vl. II
Vla.
Vlc.
Cb.
10

Wol - len wir? Wol - len wir? Un - se - re   Läm mer be - se - he!
*Will   you not? Will   you not? Our lit -tle   lambkins to   see?*___

Gelt! Komm! Komm!lieb's Bü-ber-le, komm',ich
Come, come, come, dear lad - die come, O

Er-He

bitt!" „När-ri-sches Din-ter-le, ich mag dich halt nit!"
do! Fool-ish wee las-sie I'll not go out with you!

40
Tempo I
Fl.
Ob.
Cl.
Fg.
Cor.
Trgl.
Voce
Sie-She
Willst viel-leicht --
Would you then
Tempo I
Vl.I
Vl.II
Vla.
Vlc.
Cb.
40

Etwas zurückhaltend
Fl.
Ob.
Fg.
Cor.
Voce
Willst viel leicht a bis-sel na-sche? bis-sel na-sche?
would you then a lit-tle snack have, lit-tle snack have?
arco Poco ritard.
Vl.I
Vl.II
div.
Vla.
arco
Vlc.
45
a2
Cl.
Willst viel-leicht? Willst viel-leicht? Hol' dir was aus mei-ner Tasch'!
Would you then? Would you then? Get a bite from out my sack!
Cb.
arco
50

Hol' dir was! Hol' dir was!   Hol'!
Get a bite! Get a bite!   *Get!*

Ob.
Cl.
Fg.
Voce
Vl. I
Vl. II
Vla.
Vlc.
Cb.
ten.
pizz.
Er-He
Hol'! Hol', lieb's Bü-ber-le, hol', ich bitt'!" „När-ri-sches
Get! Get it lad-die dear, get it do! Foolish wee
60
65
Cl.
Fg.
Cor.
Trgl.
Voce
Vl. I
Vl. II
Vla.
Vlc.
Cb.
poco acc.
a2
Din-ter-le, ich nasch' dir halt nit! nit!"
las-sie I no snack want from you! Not!
70

Fl.
Voce
Vl.I
Vl.II
Vla.
Vlc.
Cb.
rit.
Tempo I
Sie - She
„Gelt ich soll - -
Say, am I,
Tempo I
rit.
arco
arco
pizz.
75
Etwas zurückhaltend
Ob.
Cl.
Fg.
Cor.
Gelt? Ich soll mein Herz dir schen-ke? Herz dir schen-ke?
say, am I my heart to give then, heart to give then?
Poco ritard.
pizz.
pizz.
pizz.
div.
div.
80

Gelt? ich soll? Gelt! ich soll? Im - mer willst an mich___ ge - den - ke
Say, shall I? Say, shall I? Ev - er in your mem' - ry live___ then?

90
Ob.
a 2
p<sf>pp
Cl.
a 2
mf
1.
Fg.
Trgl.
(immer kläglicher)
(sempre più lamentevole)
Voce
Im - mer! Im - mer! Im - mer!
Ev- er, ev - er, ev - er?
Vl.I
Vl.II
Vla.
Vlc.
pizz.
arco
Cb.
pizz.
90

Nimm's! Nimm's! Nimm's, lieb's Bü - ber-le! Nimm's, ich
Take, take, take it, lad - die dear! Take it,

bitt!" ____ „När-ri-sches Din-ter-le, ich mag es halt nit! ____ nit!"
do! ____ Fool-ish wee las-sie, I don't want it of you! ____ No!"

110
Fl. picc.
Ob.
Cl.
Fg.
a 2
Cor.
a 2
Trgl.
Voce
div.
Vl.I
Vl.II
Vla.
Vlc.
pizz.
Cb.
pizz.
110

Trost im Unglück

Solace in sorrow

5
Fl.
ff
Ob.
ff
Cl.
ff
a 2
Cor.
mf
mf
a 2
Tr.
Timp.
Trgl.
f
Tbr. mil.
Vl.II
p spring. Bog.
Vla.
p saltando l'arco
Vlc.
p spring. Bog.
Ch.
5
p saltando l'arco

10
Fl. picc.
Fl.
Ob.
Cl.
Fg.
Cor.
Tr.
Trgl.
Tbr. mil.
Voce
Vl. I
Vl. II
Vla.
Vlc.
Cb.
a 2
1.
3.
pizz.
arco
Wohl -
So
10

15
Ob.
Cl.
Fg.
Cor.
Timp.
Voce
Vl.I
Vl.II
Vla.
Vlc.
Cb.
a 2
p
f
arco
an! Die Zeit ist kom-men! Mein Pferd, das muß ge - sat-telt sein! Ich
then, 'tis time for part-ing, my steed it must be sad-dled now, I've
15

hab' mir's vor-ge — nom — men! Ge — rit-ten muß es
set my mind on start - ing, a — rid-ing I must

Ob.
1.
Cl.
a 2
1.
Fg.
a 2
Tr.
a 2
Timp.
Trgl.
Tbr. mil.
Voce
sein!
go.
Geh' du nur hin!
Do thou but go,
Vl. I
Vl. II
Vla.
spring. Bog.
Vlc.
saltando l'arco
Cb.

Ich hab' mein Teil! Ich lieb' dich nur aus Nar - re-tei! Ohn'
I've had my fill, I love thee but from fol - ly still. Can

dich kann ich wohl le-ben! Ja le-ben!
part-ed go on liv-ing, yes liv-ing.

35
Fl.
Ob.
Cl.
1.2.a 2
Cor.
a 2
Tr.
Timp.
Trgl.
Tbr. mil.
mf
Voce
Ohn' dich kann ich wohl sein! So setz' ich mich aufs
With - out thee can well be! So then to horse I'll
Vl.I
Vl.II
Vla.
Vlc.
arco
Cb.
35

Pferd-chen,   und   trink' ein Gläs-chen küh-len Wein! Und schwör's bei mei-nem
blithe-ly,   and   drink a glass of spark-ling wine, and   by   my beard swear

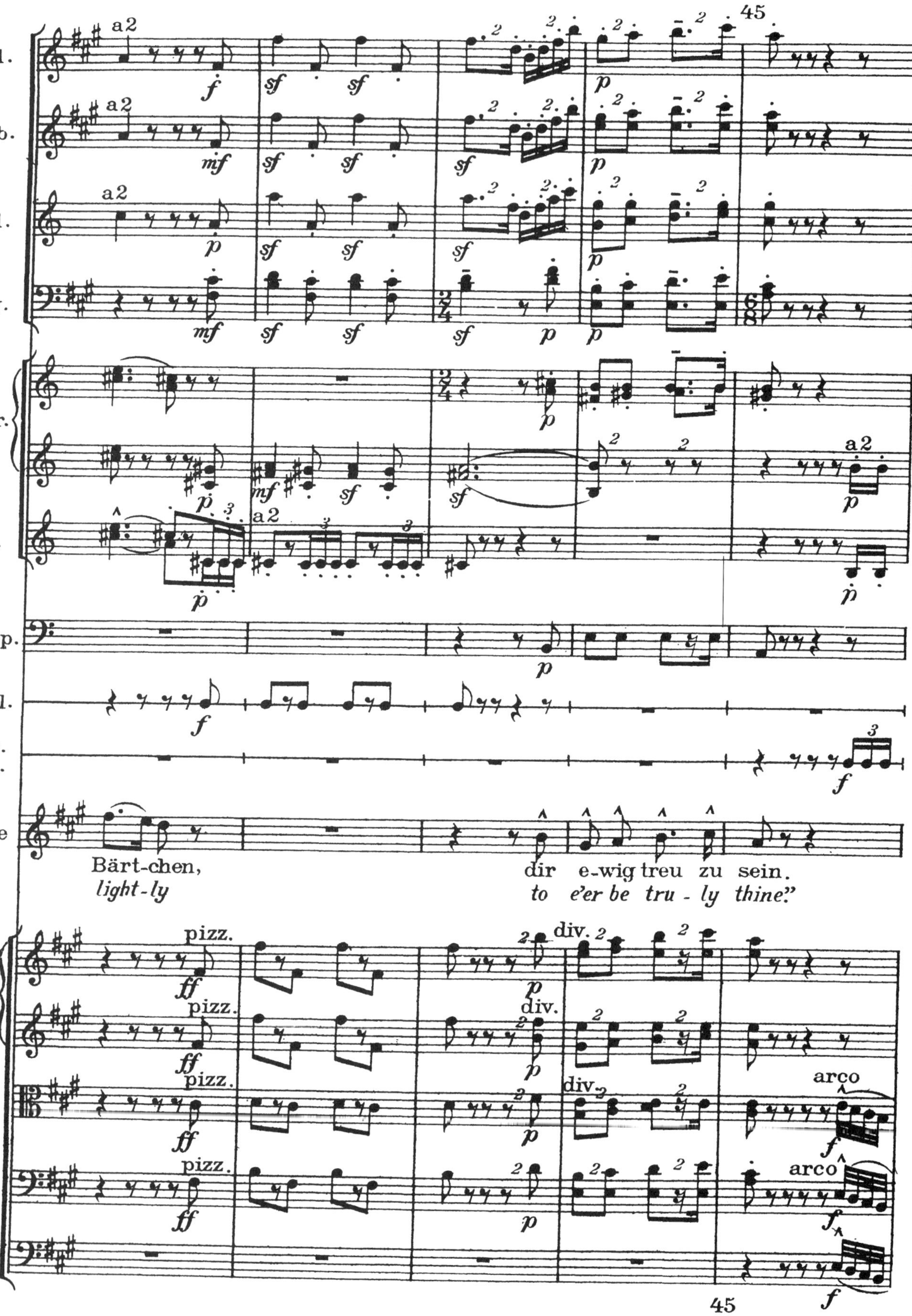
45
Fl.
Ob.
Cl.
Fg.
Cor.
Tr.
Timp.
Trgl.
Tbr. mil.
Voce
Vl. I
Vl. II
Vla.
Vlc.
Cb.
a2
pizz.
div.
arco
Bärt-chen,
light-ly
dir e-wig treu zu sein.
to e'er be tru - ly thine."
45

Fl.
Ob.
Cl.
Fg.
a2
Cor.
a2
a2
Tr.
a2
Tbr. mil.
arco
Vl.I
arco
Vl.II
Vla.
Vlc.
Cb.

50
Fl. picc.
Fl.
Ob.
Cl.
Fg.
Cor.
Trgl.
Tbr. mil.
Voce
Vl. I
Vl. II
Vla.
Vlc.
Cb.
a 2
a2
div.
espress.
Du
Dost
50

glaubst, du bist der Schön - ste wohl   auf der gan - zen   wei - ten Welt,   und
think that most ad - mir - ed thou   art the whole wide world   a - mong,   and

55

auch der An - ge - nehm - ste! Ist   a - ber weit,   weit ge fehlt!   In
cke   the most de - sir - ed, but   thou art wrong,   sad - ly wrong! With -

60

meines Vaters Gar - ten wächst ei - ne Blu - me drin! _ So
in my fa - ther's gar - den a lit - tle flow - er blows; _ so

lang will ich noch war - ten, bis die noch grö - ßer ist! _ Und
long my heart I'll hard - en un - til it larg - er grows. And

Timp.
Tbr. mil.
Voce.
geh du nur hin! Ich hab mein Teil! Ich lieb dich nur aus
do thou but go. I've had my fill, I love thee but from
springender Bogen
Vl. I
saltando l'arco
Vl. II
springender Bogen
Vla.
saltando l'arco
Vlc.
Cb.
70
Ob.
Cl.
Fg.
Cor.
Timp.
Tbr. mil.
Voce
Nar - re - tei! Ohn' dich kann ich wohl le - ben! Ohn' dich kann ich wohl
fol - ly still, can part - ed go on liv - ing, with - out thee can well
Vl. I
div.
Vl. II
Vla.
Vlc.
Cb.
75

80
Fl.
Ob.
Cl.
Fg.
a 2
Cor.
keck
con arditezza
Tr.
Timp.
Trgl.
Tbr. mil.
Voce.
sein!
be!
Vl. I
pizz.
arco
Vl. II
Vla.
Vlc.
Cb.
80

Du glaubst,ichwerd'dich neh-men! Das
Dost   think that I would take thee. Such

hab ich lang noch nicht im Sinn! Ich muß mich dei - ner   schämen!
thought as that is   far from me. A - shamed of thee wouldst make me,

Ich muß mich dei-ner schämen,wenn ich in Ge-sellschaft bin.
a - shamed of thee wouldst make me,when I am in com-pa - ny!"

100
Fl. picc.
Fl.
Ob.
Cl.
Fg.
Cor.
Tr.
Timp.
Trgl.
Tbr. mil.
Vl. I
Vl. II
Vla.
Vlc.
Cb.
a 2
ff
fff
arco
pizz.
100

Wer hat dies Liedel erdacht?

. . . Up there on the hill . . .

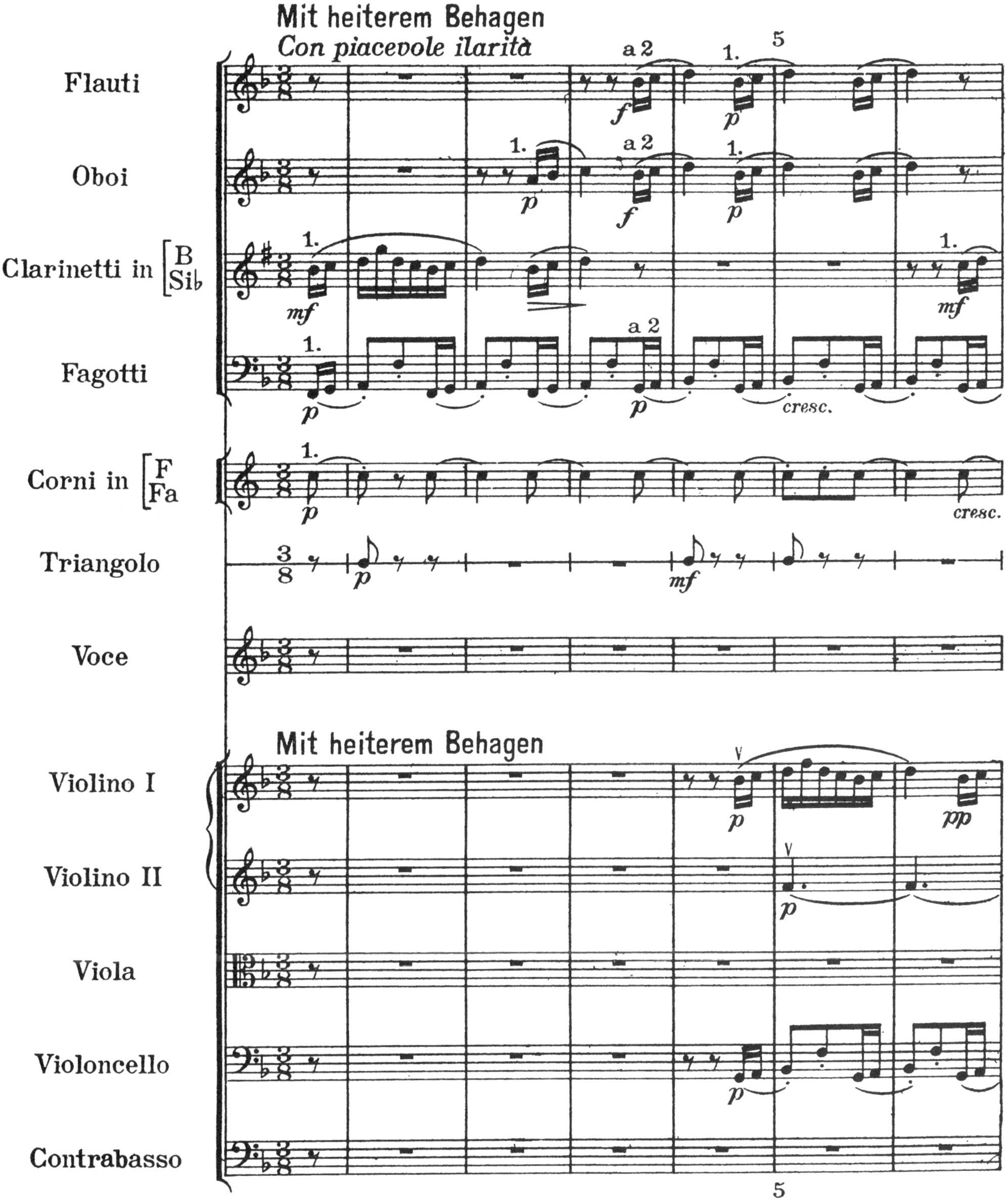

10
a tempo
Ob.
Cl.
Fg.
Cor.
Trgl.
Voce
Dort o-ben am
Up there on the
a tempo
Vl.I
Vl.II
Vla.
Vlc.
Cb.
pizz.
10

15
20
Fl.
Ob.
Cl.
Fg.
Cor.
Trgl.
Voce
Vl. I
Vl. II
Vla.
Vlc.
Cb.
hervor-
rile-
Berg in dem ho - hen Haus, in dem Haus,
hill in the house so high, house so high!
da
At
arco
arco
pizz.
pizz.
pizz.
pizz.
pizz.

tretend
1. vato
Ob.
Cl.
Fg.
Trgl.
Voce
guk-ket ein fein's, lieb's Mä-del her - aus. Es ist nicht dort da -
win-dow a dear, sweet las - sie I spy. 'T is not her home up
Vl.I
Vl.II
Vla.
Vlc.
Cb.
arco
25
Voce
hei-me! Es ist nicht dort da - hei-me! Es ist des Wirts sein
yon-der! 'T is not her home up yon-der! She is the old inn -
Vl.I
Vl.II
Vla.
Vlc.
Cb.
pizz.
30

a 2
Cor.
Trgl.
Voce
Töch - ter- lein. Es woh-net auf grü - ner Hai
keep - er's lass! She dwell-eth where green the heath
Vl.I
Vl.II
arco
Vla.
Vlc.
arco
Cb.
35
a 2
Cor.
Trgl.
Voce
Vl.I
Vl.II
pizz.
Vla.
pizz.
Vlc.
pizz.
Cb.
40

Gemächlich
Comodo
Ob.
Cl.
Fg.
Cor.
a 2
Trgl.
Voce
de. Mein Herz - le — ist wund. Komm',
er! My heart is — full sore! Come,
Gemächlich
Vl. I
Vl. II
Vla.
Vlc.
Cb.
pizz.
45
Schätz - le, — mach's g'sund! Dein schwarz-brau - ne — Äug - lein, die
sweet, it — re - store! Thy spark - ling brown eyes they have
arco
div.
50

Ob. Cl. Fg. Cor. Voce Vl.I Vl.II Vla. Vlc. Cb.

hab'n mich ver - wund't! Dein ro - si - ger Mund macht Her - zen ge -
wound-ed me sore! Thy lips' hon - ey store will cure hearts once

55

Fl. Ob. Cl. Fg. Voce Vl.I Vl.II Vla. Vlc.

sund. Macht Ju - gend ver - stän - dig, macht To - te le - ben - dig, macht
more, make young quit their sigh - ing, new life give the dy - ing, make

60

65
Fl.
Ob.
Cl.
Fg.
Cor.
Trgl.
Voce
Kran-ke ge - sund, macht Kran-ke ge - sund, ja ge - sund. Wer
sick well once more, make sick well once more, yes, once more. Who
Vl. I
Vl. II
Vla.
Vlc.
Cb.
a 2
cresc.
arco
pizz.
65

Ob.
Cl.
Ptti.
Voce
Vl. I
Vl. II
Vla.
Vlc.
Cb.
1.
hervortretend
rilevato
pizz.
hat denn das schön schö - ne Lied - lein er - dacht? Es ha-ben's drei
was it of this lit - tle dit - ty had thought? It was by three
70
Fg.
Cor.
Gäns' ü - bers Was-ser ge - bracht! Zwei grau-e und ei-ne wei-ße, zwei
geese o'er the wa - ter once brought. Two gray ones and a white one! Two
75

Ob.
Fg.
Cor.
Trgl.
Voce
Vl. I
Vl. II
Vla.
Vlc.
Cb.
1.
a 2
grau-e und ei-ne wei-ße! Und wer das Lied-lein nicht sin-gen kann, dem
gray ones and a white one! And he who this dit-ty can't sing, for him to
wol-len sie es pfei-fen! Ja!
whis-tle it they're wil-ling! Yes
pizz.
arco
div.
cresc.
80
85
90

95
Fl.
Ob.
Cl.
Fg.
a 2
Cor.
a 2
Trgl.
Voce
Vl.I
Vl.II
Vla.
pizz.
Vlc.
pizz.
Cb.
pizz.
95

Das irdische Leben

Earthly life

10
Fl.
Ob.
Cor. ingl.
Cl.
1.
Fg.
Tr.
mit beängstigtem Ausdruck
con espressione straziante
Voce
„Mut - ter, ach Mut - ter, es hun - gert mich!
„Mot - her, o Mot - her so hung - ry— I,
Vl. I
Vl. II
Vla.
Vlc.
10

Fl.
Ob.
Cor. ingl.
Cl.
Fg.
Cor.
Tr.
Voce
a 2
Gib mir Brot, sonst ster - be ich."
give me bread or I shall die!"
Vl. I
Vl. II
Vla.
Vlc.
arco
pizz.
div.

15
Ob.
Cl.
Voce
Vl. I
Vl. II
Vla.
Vlc.
ff
p
f
(p)
„War - te nur!
„Wait a while!
pp
pizz.
pizz.
15

War- te nur, mein lie - bes Kind! Mor - gen wol - len wir
Wait a while, my dar - ling o, we to - mor - row

ern - ten ge - schwind!"
rea - ping will go:"

30
Fl.
Cor. ingl.
Cl.
Voce
Und als das Korn ge-
When the_ corn was
Vl. I
Vl. II
Vla.
Vlc.
Cb.
30

35
Fl.
Ob.
ppp
Cor. ingl.
pp
2.
Cl.
pp
Voce
ern - tet war, rief das Kind noch im - mer -
rea - ped next sun, still the child's sad cry went
Vl. I
Vla.
Vlc.
35

40
a 2
Fl.
Ob.
Cor. ingl.
Cl.
Voce
espr.
dar: „Mut - ter, ach Mut - ter, es hun - gert mich!
on: „Mot - her, o Mot - her, so hung - ry— I,
Vl. I
Vl. II
Vla.
Vlc.
Cb.
40

45
Fl.
pp
Ob.
1.
f
Cor. ingl.
p
Cl.
1.
f
con sord.
Tr.
ffp
Voce
f
f
Gib mir Brot, sonst ster - be ich!“
give me bread or I shall die!“
Vl.I
pp
f
p
f
p
div.
pp
f
p
f
p
p
Vl.II
Vla.
p
ff
p
p
ff
p
pp
Vlc.
p
ff
p
p
ff
p
Cb.
45

50
Ob.
Cor. ingl.
Cl.
Tr.
Voce
(p)
„War-te nur! War-te nur, mein
„Wait a while, wait a while, my
Vl. I
Vl. II
Vla.
Vlc.
50

55
Cor. ingl.
Voce
lie - bes Kind! Mor - gen wol - len wir dro - schen ge -
dar - ling o, we to - mor - row thras-hing will
Vl. I
Vl. II
Vla.
espr.
Vlc.
55

60
a2
1.
Fl.
Ob.
Cor. ingl.
Cl.
Voce
schwind!“
go.“
spr. Bogen
saltando l'arco
spr. Bogen
saltando l'arco
Vl. I
Vl. II
Vla.
Vlc.
Cb.
60

65
Cor. ingl.
Cl.
Voce
Und als das Korn ge - dro - schen
When the_ corn was thras-hed next
Vl. I
div.
Vl. II
arco
Vla.
Vlc.
Cb.
65

70
Ob.
Cor. ingl.
Cl.
a2
pp
Voce
war, rief das Kind noch im - mer - dar:
sun, still the child's sad cry went on:
Vl. I
Vl. II
Vla.
Vlc.
f
pp
ff
f > pp
ff > pp
p
70

75
Fl.
Ob.
Cor. ingl.
a2
Cl.
Fg.
Voce
Mut - ter, ach Mut - ter, es hun - gert mich, gib mir
„Mot - her, o Mot - her, so hung - ry I, give me
Vl. I
espr.
Vl. II
Vla.
Vlc.
arco
div. arco
Cb.
75

Brot, sonst ster - be ich!"
bread or I shall die!"

85
a 2
Fl.
1.
Ob.
Cor. ingl.
p
a 3 +
Cor.
ffp
Tr.
Voce
(p)
„War-te nur! War-te nur, mein lie - bes
„Wait a while, wait a while, my dar - ling
Vl. I
pp
spr. Bogen
saltando l'arco
pp
Vl. II
pizz.
p
pizz.
p
Vla.
pp
pp
pizz.
p
Vlc.
pp
pp
pp
pizz.
p
Cb.
pizz.
p
p
85

90
1.
Fl.
Cor. ingl.
Voce
Kind! Mor - gen wol - len wir bak - ken ge-schwind!"
o, we to - mor - row — ba - king will go."
spr. Bogen
saltando l'arco
Vl. I
Vl. II
arco
Vla.
arco
Vlc.
spr. Bogen
saltando l'arco
arco
pizz.
Cb.
90

95
1.
Fl.
mf
p
1.
Ob.
ppp
Cl.
pp
Vl. I
p
pp
pp
Vl. II
4a corda
arco
mf
pizz.
p
Vla.
pizz.
pp
pizz.
f
Vlc.
pizz.
Cb.
95

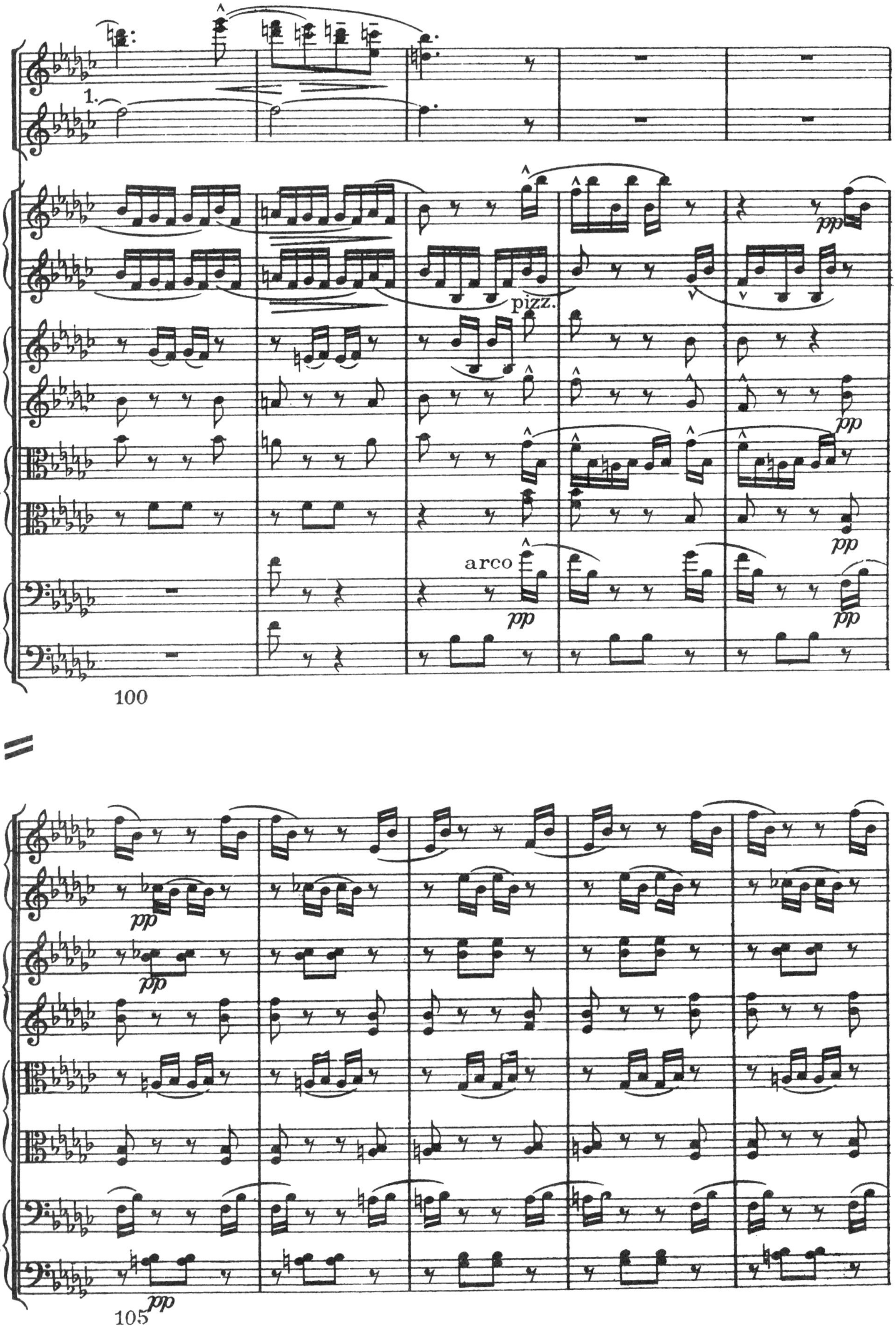
Fl.
Ob.
1.
Vl. I
Vl. II
Vla.
Vlc.
pizz.
arco
pp
100
105

Etwas zögernd
Poco esitando
110
Fl.
Cor. ingl.
Cl.
Cor.
Voce
Und als das Brot ge - bak - ken war,
And when the bread was ba - ked next day,
Etwas zögernd
Vl.I
Vl.II
Vla.
Vlc.
110

115
a 2
Fl.
pp
Ob.
p ausdrucksvoll
espressivo
Cor. ingl.
pp
Fg.
p
a 2
p
Cor.
fp
Voce
lag
cold
das
the
Vl. I
p
Vl. II
arco
pp
Vla.
p
arco
Vlc.
p
arco
p
115

120
a 2
Fl.
Ob.
Cor. ingl.
Cl.
Fg.
Cor.
Tr.
Voce.
Kind auf der To - - - ten - - - bahr!
child in the cof - - - fin lay!
Vl.I
Vl.II
arco
Vla.
Vlc.
120

a 2
125
Fl.
fffp
ff
p
Ob.
a 2
Cor. ingl.
Cl.
Fg.
Cor.
fp
pp
Tr.
Voce
Vl. I
f
mf
4a corda
Vl. II
Vla.
Vlc.
arco
Cb.

Cl.
Fg.
Cor.
Ptti.
Vl.I
Vl.II
Vla.
Vlc.
Cb.
a 2
a 2
1.
130
135
mit Schwammschlägel
con bacchette di spugna
pizz.
130
135

Des Antonius von Padua Fischpredigt

Antonius of Padua's fish sermon

English version by
Addie Funk

Fg.

Voce

to _ nius zur Pre-digt die Kir _ che find't le _ dig! Er geht zu den
to _ nius for ser - vice the church finds de _ ser - ted! He goes to the

Vl. I

Vla. pizz.

Vlc.

10

Cl.

Fg. 3.

Trgl.

Voce

Flüs-sen und pre-digt den Fi _ schen! Sie schlag mit den Schwänzen! Im
ri - vers to preach to the fi - shes! They all come a - swimming in the

Vl. I

Vl. II pizz.

Vla.

Vlc.

15

Cl.
Fg.
Trgl.
Voce
3.
2.
3.
p
Son-nen-schein glän-zen! Im Son-nen-schein, Son-nen-schein glän-zen, sie
sun-shine a - glea-ming, the sun-shine, the sun-shine a - glea-ming, a -
20
pp
ppp
Timp.
R.
Vl. I
Vl. II
Vla.
Vlc.
Cb.
glän-zen, sie glän-zen, glän-zen! Die Karp-fen mit
glea-ming, a - glea-ming, glea-ming! The carp something
arco
25

Voce
Vl. I
Vla.
Vlc.
Cb.
Ro - gen sind all' hier - her zo - gen, hab'n d'Mäu - ler auf - ris - sen, sich
no - ting in shoals come a - floa - ting with mouth wide a - sun - der they
30
Cl.
Fg.
Voce
Vl. I
Vl. II
Vla.
Vlc.
Cb.
Zu - hörn's be - flis - sen!
lis - ten in won - der.
p
2.
pizz.
35
40

45
Fl.
Ob.
Cl.
Fg.
Voce
Kein Pre-digt nie - ma-len
Fish ne'- er like the pre-sent
den
found
Vl.I
Vl.II
arco
Vla.
Vlc.
Cb.
45

Ob.
Cl.
Fg.
Voce
Vl.I
Vl.II
Vla.
Vlc.
Cb.
1.
mit Humor
con umore
1.2.
Fi-schen so g'fal-len!
ser-mon so plea-sant!
pizz.
50
Fl.
in A-La
in B-Si♭
3.
pizz.
55

Spitz-
And

arco

go-sche - te Hech - te, die im - mer - zu fech - ten, sind ei - lends her-
pike so sharp snou - ted who o - thers have rou - ted in num - bers come

schwom-men, zu hö - ren den From-men! Auch je - ne Phan - ta -sten, die
spee - ding to the Ho - ly Man's rea - ding. The bi - got-ted e - ven, for

Cl.

Fg.

Cor.

Timp.

Voce

im - mer-zu   fa - sten: die Stock-fisch ich   mei - ne, zur Pre-digt er -
fas - ting much   gi - ven: to   cod   I'm   al - lu - ding, their heads are   pro-

Vl. I

Vl. II

Vla.

Vlc.

Cb.

80
Fl.
Ob.
Cl.
Fg.
Cor.
Trgl.
R.
Voce
scheinen.
tru-ding!
Kein Predigt nie - ma-len
Cod ne'- er like the pre-sent
Vl.I
Vl.II
Vla.
Vlc.
Cb.
arco
pizz.
80

85
90
Fl.
Ob.
Cl.
Fg.
Cor.
Trgl.
R.
Voce
Vl.I
Vl.II
Vla.
Vlc.
Cb.
mit Parodie
con parodia
den Stockfisch so g'fal-len!
found ser-mon so pleasant!
pizz.
pizz.

95
Fl.
Ob.
Cl.
Fg.
Cor.
Ptti.
Vl. I
Vl. II
Vla.
Vlc.
Cb.
1. stacc.
2. stacc.
a 2
Becken mit Schwammsch.
Piatti con bacchette di spugna
(verklingen lassen)
(lasci lentamente spegnere)
arco
div.
95

100
Cl.
p
p
Fg.
mf
a 2
mf
Cor.
1.3. a 2
mf
2.4. a 2
mf
Timp.
p
Ptti.
Tamt.
p
Vl. II
Vla.
f
pp
p
Vlc.
arco
mf
p
Cb.
pizz.
mf
p
100

Gut Aa - le und
Proud sal-mon so

105

Hau-sen, die vor-neh-me schmausen, die selbst sich be - que - men, die
ab - le to grace rich man's tab - le with mien con-des - cen-ding are

110

Cl.
pppp
Fg.
pppp
Cor.
2.
ppp
Voce
Pre-digt ver - neh-men! Auch Kreb - se, Schild-kro-ten, sonst lang - sa-me
al - so at - ten-ding. While crabs, too, and turt - le ex - ci - ted-ly
Vla.
p
Vlc.
Cb.
115
Ob.
1.
p
Fg.
p
Cor.
2.
p
1.
p
Voce
(cantabile)
Bo-ten, stei-gen ei - lig vom Grund, zu hö-ren die-sen Mund!
hurt-le, el - se slow in their ways, to hear what he__ says.
Vl. I
pp
Vl. II
pp
Vla.
pizz.
arco
pp
Vlc.
pp
Cb.
120

Fg.

Cor. 1.

Voce

Kein Pre-digt nic - ma-len   den
Crabs ne'er like   the   pre-sent   found

Vl. I.

Vl. II.

Vla.

Vlc.

125   130

Ob.

Cl.

Fg.

Cor.

Timp.

R.

Ptti.

Voce

Stockfisch so   g'fal-len! Fisch   gro - ße,Fisch' klei-ne, vor- nehmundge-
ser - mon so   plea-sant! Fish   small and fish   grea-ter, proud, humb-le by

Vl. I.

Vl. II.

Vla.

Vlc.

Cb.

135

mei-ne, er - he-ben die Köp-fe wie ver-ständ'ge Ge-schöpfe!
na-ture, at - ten-tive-ly   lis-ten   li - ke crea-tures with rea-son!

Auf Got - tes Be - geh-ren   die Pre-digt an -
O - bey - ing God's wis-hes   *that His words hear the*

150
Fl.
Ob.
1.
mit Humor
con umore
Cl.
Fg.
2.
Cor.
Voce
hören!
fish-es.
pizz.
Vl.I
Vl.II
Vla.
Vlc.
Cb.
150

155
Fl.
Ob.
Cl.
Fg.
Cor.
a 2
mit Schwammschl.
con bacchette di spugna
Ptti.
Gr.C.
div. arco
Vl.I
Vl.II
Vla.
Vlc.
arco
Cb.
155

Cl.
mf
mf
Voce
Die Pre-digt ge - en-det, ein je - der sich
When ser - mon is en - ded all turn who at -
Vla.
pp spicc.
sempre stacc.
Vlc.
pp spicc.
sempre stacc.
Cb.
pp spicc.
160
sempre stacc.
Fl.
1.
p
Ob.
1.
p
Cl.
mf
Fg.
1.
mf
Voce
wen-det.
ten - ded!
Die
The
Vl. I
pp
pp
Vl. II
pp
Vla.
Vlc.
Cb.
165

Ob.
Cl.
Voce
Vl.I
Vl.II
Vla.
Vlc.
Cb.
1.
f
Hech - te bleiben Die - be, die Aa - le viel lie - ben; die Pre - digt hat
pike fall to prey - ing, the sal - mon to play - ing, the ser - mon, though
pp
sempre stacc.
170
pizz.
Fl.
1.
a 2
p espress.
g'fal - len, sie blei - ben wie Al - len! Die Krebs geh'n zu - rük - ke; die
plea - sant, their faults has not les - sened. The crabs all go back - ward, the
gliss.
div.
175
p arco

180
a 2
Fl.
a 2
Ob.
1.
Cl.
1. 2.
Fg.
3.
Timp.
Voce
Stock-fisch'bleib'n dik-ke, die Kar-pfen viel fres-sen, die Pre-digt ver-
cod re - main awk-ward, the carp still a— glut-ton has ser-mon for-
Vl. I
Vl. II
pizz.
Vla.
arco
arco
div.
Vlc.
pizz.
pizz.
Cb.
180
pizz.

185
a 2
Fl.
ff
1.
Ob.
f
f
Cl.
f
mf
mf
Fg.
f
f
1.3. a 2
2.4. a 2
Cor.
ff
ff
Timp.
mit Schwammschl.
con bacchette di spugna
Ptti.
ff
Voce
ges-sen, ver-ges-sen! Die Pre - digt hat g'fal-len, sie blei - ben wie
got-ten, for-got-ten! Their faults are not les-sened by ser-mon, though
pizz.
Vl. I
cresc.
f
ff
pizz.
Vl. II
cresc.
f
ff
pizz.
Vla.
ff
pizz.
Vlc.
ff
Cb.
185

Al-len, die Predigt hat g'fallen, hat g'fallen!
pleasant, their faults are not les-sened, not les-sened!

Rheinlegendchen

Little legend of the Rhine

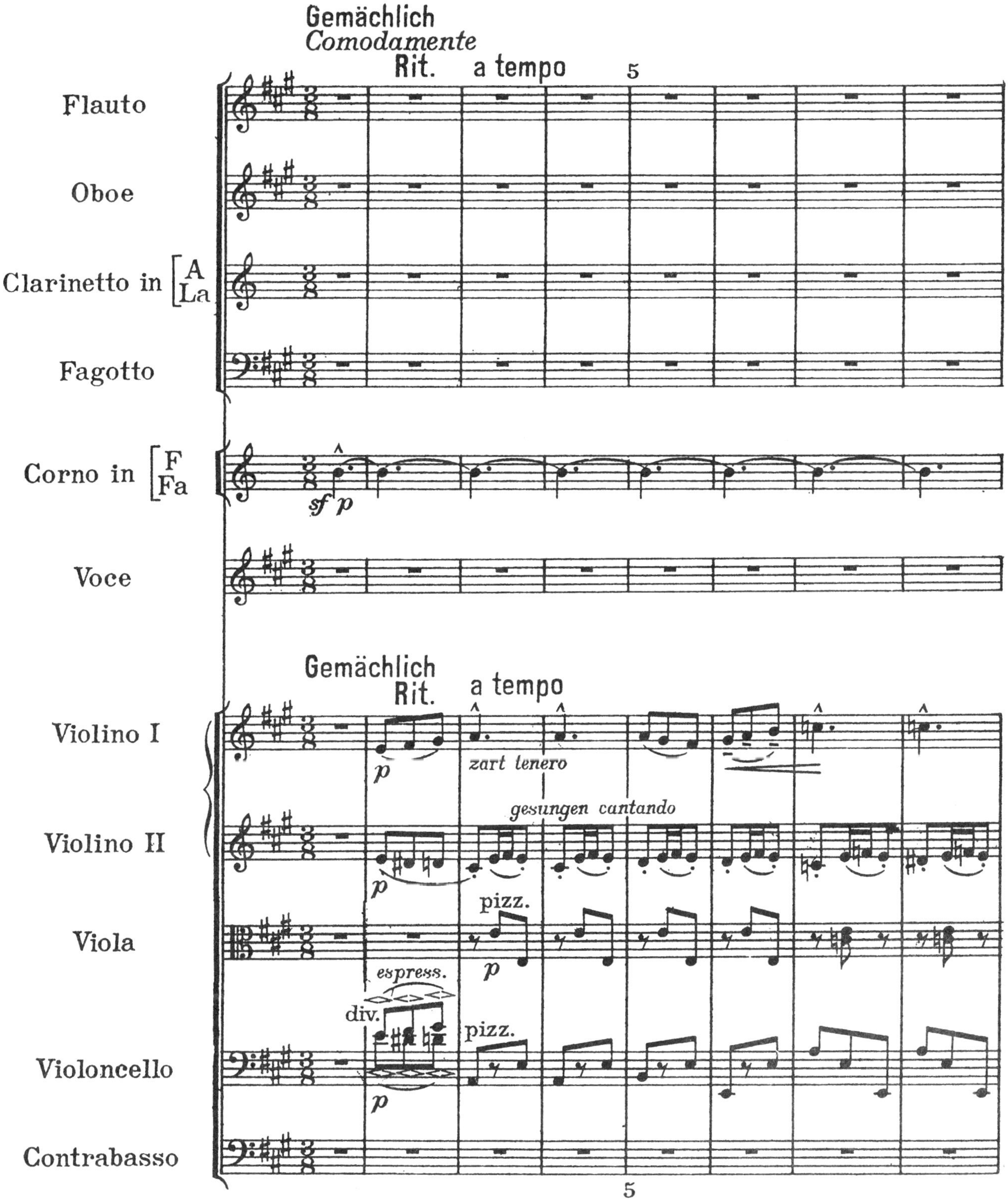

poco rit.
Rit.
Fl.
Ob.
Cl.
Fg.
Cor.
Vl. I
Vl. II
Vla.
Vlc.
poco rit.
dim.
10
15
a tempo
Voce
Bald gras' ich am Nek-kar, bald gras' ich am Rhein; bald
I — mow by the Neck-ar, a - non by — the Rhine, at
a tempo
arco
20

hab' ich ein Schät-zel, bald bin ich al - lein! Was hilft mir das
times I've a sweet-heart, at times none is mine! What good is my

pizz. 25

Gra-sen, wenn d'Si-chel nicht schneid't! Was hilft mir ein Schät-zel, wenn's
sick - le if sharp it not be,— what good is a sweet-heart who

30

bei mir nicht bleïbt!
stays not with me!

So soll ich denn gra-sen am Nek-kar, am
Now if by the Neck-ar, the Rhine I___ must

Rhein, so werf' ich mein gol - de - nes Ring - lein hin - ein.
mow, my lit - tle gold ring in their wa - ters I'll throw!

Es flie - ßet im Nek - kar und flie - ßet im Rhein, soll
'Twill float in the Neck - ar, 'twill float in the Rhine, a

schwimmen hin - un-ter ins Meer tief hin - ein.
swim-ming will float out to o - cean's deep brine!

rit.
a tempo
Fl.
Ob.
Cl.
Fg.
Cor.
p espr.
Voce
Und schwimmt es, das Ring-lein, so
And swim - ming the ring will be
arco
Vl.I
Vl.II
Vla.
Vlc.
Cb.
pizz.
70
(ein wenig gemäßigter als im Anfang)
(un poco più moderato che il principio)
frißt es ein Fisch! Das Fisch - lein soll kom-men aufs Kö - nigs sein
gulped by a fish! The fish for king's ta - ble be served a good
75

Tisch!   Der   Kö - nig   tät   fra - gen: wem's Ring-lein sollt' sein?
dish!   The   king   he   will   que - ry   whose   may   the   ring   be?

85
zart hervortretend
teneramente rilevato
molto rit.
a tempo
Fl.
Ob.
Cl.
Fg.
Cor.
Voce
Da tät mein Schatz sa-gen: Das
My sweet-heart will say: It be-
Vl.-S.
Vl. I
Vl. II
Vla.
Vlc.
Cb.
p
ppp
p subito
pizz.
arco
p espr.
85

rit.
(sogleich etwas zurückhalten)
(subito poco ritard.)
90
molto rit.
a tempo (wie im Anfang)
(come il principio)
Fl.
Ob.
Cl.
Fg.
Cor.
molto espr.
Voce
Ring-lein g'hört mein.
long-eth to me!
Mein
My
Vl.-S.
Vl. I
Vl. II
Vla.
Vlc.
Cb.
molto cresc.
pochett. rit.
arco
div.
molto espr.
90

Schätz-lein tät sprin - gen Berg auf und Berg ein,_ tät mir wied-rum
sweet-heart will hast - en_ o'er mount - ain and glen_ and bring me my

brin - gen das Gold - ring-lein mein!_
lit - tle gold ring back a - gain!_

(ohne Nachschlag *senza aggiuntazione*)

Kannst gra - sen am Nek - kar, kannst gra - sen am
So then by the Neck - ar,— the— Rhine thou mayst

Rhein! Wirf du mir nur im - mer dein Ring - lein hin - ein!
mow, if but in their wa - ters thy ring thou wilt throw!

115
120
Fl.
Ob.
Cl.
Fg.
Cor.
Vl.I
div.
Vl.II
Vla.
pizz.
Vlc.
arco
pizz.
Cb.
115
120

Lied des Verfolgten im Turm

Song of the persecuted man in the tower

ra - ten,   sie rau-schen vor-bei wie nächt-li-che Schatten,
tec - tors,   *they rush by and flee like sha-do-wy spect-res,*

5
a 2
Ob.
cresc.
fp
molto cresc.
Cl.
Fg.
f
Cor.
p
cresc.
Timp.
tr
pp
Voce
kein Mensch kann sie wis - - sen, kein Jäger sie
no per - son can know them, no hunter lay
Vl.I
Vl.II
Vla.
Vlc.
Cb.

Ob.
a 2
Cl.
Fg.
a 2
Cor.
Timp.
Voce
schie - - ßen, es blei-bet da - bei, es blei-bet da-bei, die Ge-
low_____ them, it is and shall be, it is and shall be: our
Vl.I
Doppelgr.
doppie corde
Vl.II
4a corda
Vla.
div.
Vlc.
Cb.
pizz.

a 2
10
1.
Fl.
Ob.
Cl.
Fg.
Cor.
Tr.
Timp.
Voce
Vl.I
Vl.II
Vla.
Vlc.
Cb.
con sord.
pizz.
dim.
danken sind frei!
thouhts they are free!

Fl.
Ob.
Cl.
Fg.
Tr.
Voce
Vl.I
Vl.II
Vla.
Vlc.
Cb.
Das Mädchen The Maiden
Im Som - - mer ist gut lu - - stig sein auf
In sum - - mer it must plea - - sant be on
a 2
Doppelgr.
doppie corde
div.
pizz.
arco
div.
pizz.
div.

Fl.
Ob.
Cl.
Fg.
Voce
Vl.I
Vl.II
Vla.
Vlc.
a 2
1.
ho - hen,wil - den Ber - gen.
hill - topsgrown with hea - ther.
Dort
There
con sord.
con sord.
con sord.
div.
pizz.
con sord
15
fin - det man grün' Plät - ze-lein, mein Herz ver-lieb - tes
would I find green nooks for thee my heart's own love, O
leggiero sempre
leggiero
20

a 2
Fl.
Ob.
p
sf
pp
1.
Cl.
p
Fg.
p
sf
pp
Cor.
sf p
4.
p
Voce
sf
Schät - ze-lein, von dir, von dir mag ich nicht
come with me, from thee, from thee I would not
Vl.I
sf
sf
pp
Vl.II
tr
gliss.
sf
pp
Vla.
pp
Vlc.
pp
sf
pp leggiero
pizz.
Cb.
p

25
a2
1.
a2
1.
1.
Fl.
Ob.
Cl.
Fg.
Cor.
Voce
schei - den.
se - ver!
Vl.I
Vl.II
Vla.
Vlc.
Cb.
pp
tr
senza sord.
senza sord.
25

Fl.
Ob.
Cl.
Fg.
Cor.
Tr.
Voce
Vl.I
Vl.II
Vla.
Vlc.
Cb.
a 2
1.
30
con sord.
Der Gefangene - The Prisoner
Und sperrt man mich ein in fin-ste-re
And though I be locked in dungeon for-
4a corda
div.
pizz.
arco

Ob.
a 2
Cl.
a 2
Fg.
Cor.
Voce
Ker - ker, dies al-les sind nur, dies al-les sind nur ver-geb-li-che
ev er, it all is in-vain, it all is in-vain and fruitless en-
Vl.I
senza sord.
Vl.II
senza sord.
4a corda
Vla.
Vlc.
Cb.

Fl.
a 2
ff
Ob.
a 2
Cl.
a 2
Fg.
a 2
Cor.
fp
cresc.
fp
cresc.
fp
cresc.
fp
cresc.
Timp.
tr
pp
cresc.
f
Voce
Wer - ke, denn mei-ne Ge - dan - - ken zer-rei-ßen die
dea - vour; my thoughts still had ris - - en o'er walls of my
Vl.I
Vl.II
Vla.
trem.
fp
molto cresc.
ff
Vlc.
mf
molto cresc.
f
Cb.
mf
molto cresc.
ff

Schran - ken und Mau-ern ent-zwei, die Gedan-ken sind frei,   die Ge-
pri - son and shat-tered its key, our thoughts they are free!   *Our*

Fl.
Ob.
Cl.
Fg.
Cor.
Tr.
Timp.
Voce
Vl.I
Vl.II
Vla.
Vlc.
Cb.
a 2
ff
f
p
pp
senza sord.
tr
Das Mädchen - The Maiden
dan - ken sind frei!
thoughts they are free!
Im
In

a 2
Fl.
pp
sempre pp
1.2.
Cor.
p
Voce
Som - mer ist gut lu - stig sein, gut lu - stig sein auf
sum - mer it must plea - sant be, must plea - sant be on
Vl. I
cantabile
Vl. II
pp
pizz.
Vla.
p
pizz.
Vlc.
40
a 2
Fl.
Ob.
pp
Cl.
p
1.2.
Cor.
Voce
ho - hen, wil - den Ber - - - - - - -
moun - tains high and lof - - - - - - -
Vl. I
Vl. II
Vla.

a 2
Fl.
Ob.
Cl.
Fg.
1.2.
Cor.
Voce
gen.
ty.
Man ist da
A - lone we
Vl.I
Vl.II
Vla.
sempre pizz.
Vlc.
45
Fl.
Ob.
1.
Cl.
Fg.
Voce
e - wig ganz al - lein auf ho - hen wil - den Ber -
there would al - ways be on moun - tains high and lof -
Vla.
Vlc.
50

gen, man hört da gar kein Kin-der-ge - schrei, kein Kin-der-ge -
ty, there naught is heard of chil-dren's cries, of chil-dren's

schrei!
cries!

Die Luft mag ei - nem da
The air may breathe there in

55

Fl.
Ob.
Fg.
Voce
Vl.I
Vl.II
Vla.
Vlc.
1.
p
wer - den, ja, die Luft mag ei - nem wer - - - -
safe - ty, yes, the air may breathe in safe - - - -
60
Fl.
Ob.
Cl.
Tr.
Timp.
Voce
Vl.I
Vl.II
Vla.
Vlc.
Cb.
dim.
senza sord.
f
Der Gefangene - The Prisoner
ff
den. So sei's wie es sei, und wenn es sich
ty. Then let it be so, and if for-tune
pp
morendo
div.
65

Fl.
Ob.
Cl.
Cor.
Tr.
Timp.
Voce.
Vl.I
Vl.II
Vla.
Vlc.
Cb.
a 2
ff
f
mf
div.
schik - ket, nur al - les, al - les sei in der Stil - le, nur all's in der
fa - vors, but all done, all done soft - ly and low, but all soft and

Still, all's in der Still!
low, all soft and low.

70
Fl.
Ob.
a 2
mf
Cl.
a 2
mf
Fg.
a 2
a 2
mf
Cor.
mf
a 2
mf
Tr.
a 2
f
Timp.
f
Voce
ff
Mein Wunsch und Be - geh - ren, nie-mand kann's
A wish that is hid - den can't be for -
Vla.
3
Vlc.
70

weh - ren!
bid - den!

Es bleibt da-bei: die Ge-dan-ken sind frei, die Ge-dan-ken sind
It is and shall be: our thoughts they are free, our thoughts they are

75
Ob.
a 2
ff
Cl.
a 2
ff
Fg.
ff
Cor.
sff
sff
mf
sf
sf
Timp.
p
Voce
frei!
free.
Vl.I
Vl.II
Vla.
pizz.
f
Vlc.
p
Cb.
p
75

Fl.
Ob.
Cl.
Fg.
Cor.
Tr.
Timp.
Voce
Vl.I
Vl.II
Vla.
Vlc.
Cb.
1.
a 2
4a corda
pizz.
Das Mädchen - The Maiden
Mein Schatz, du singst so
My love, dost sing as

Fl.
Ob.
Cl.
Cor.
Voce
Vl.I
Vla.
Vlc.
1.
fröh-lich hier, wie's Vö - ge-lein im Gra - - - - -
mer-ri - ly, as bird a-mong the bran - - - - -
p
80
Fl.
Cl.
Fg.
Cor.
Voce
Vl.I
Vla.
Vlc.
- - - se.
- - - ches;
pp
arco
div.
85

a 2
Fl.
1.
Ob.
p
pp
a 2
Cl.
p
Fg.
pp
Voce
Ich steh' so trau-rig bei
At pri - son door I stand
Vl. I
ppp
tr
arco
pizz.
Vl. II
p
pp
arco
pp
Vla.
pizz.
pp
arco
pp
pizz.
Vlc.
p
pizz.
Cb.
pp

Ker - ker-tür, wär' ich doch tot, wär' ich bei dir, ach
mourn - ful-ly, were I but dead were I with thee, ah

muß, _____ ach muß ich im - mer denn kla - gen!?
must, _____ ah must I ev - er be griev - ing?

95

Der Gefangene - The Prisoner

Und weil du so klagst,
And since thou mak'st moan,

der Lieb' ich ent-
all love I'll be

sa - ge! Und ist es ge-wagt, und ist es gewagt, so kann mich nichts
leav - ing! *And when it is done, and when it is done no lon-ger be*

pla - gen! So kann ich im Her - - zen stets lachen und
griev - ing! In heart hold here - af - - ter but jest-ing and

105
Fl.
Ob.
Cl.
Fg.
Cor.
Timp.
Voce
Vl. I
Vl. II
Vla.
Vlc.
Cb.
a 2
ohne Nachschlag
senza aggiunzione
4ª corda
arco
pizz.
scher - - zen. Es blei-bet da - bei, es blei-bet da-bei, die Ge-
laugh - - ter. It is and shall be, it is and shall be: Our
105

Fl.
Ob.
Cl.
Fg.
Cor.
Tr.
Timp.
Voce
Vl. I
Vl. II
Vla.
Vlc.
Cb.
a 2
ff
fp
con sord. a 2
dan-ken sind frei!
thoughts they are free!
4a corda
pizz.

Die Ge - dan - ken sind frei!
Our— thoughts they are free!

Wo die schönen Trompeten blasen

Where the beautiful trumpets blow

Fl.
Ob.
Cl.
Cor.
Tr.
Vla.
Vlc.
1.
ppp
pp
1. con sord.
mf
sfpp
15
Poco ritard.
3.
Voce
Wer ist denn drau-ßen und wer klop-fet an, der
Who is it knocks there and who can it be that
20

1.
Fl.
p
Ob.
pp
Cl.
1. sempre con sord.
Tr.
Voce
mich so lei - se, so lei - se wek - ken kann!?
doth so soft - ly, so soft - ly wa - ken me?
25
30
poco rit.
sf
sempre con sord.
Cor.
a 2
ppp
Das
Have
Vl. I
Vl. II
35

Voce
Vl.I
Vl.II
Vla.
Vlc.
Cb.
ist der Herz-al-ler-lieb-ste dein, steh' auf und laß mich zu dir
e'er thy heart'sbestbe-lo-ved been, get up and let me to thee
pp
pp
div.
pp pizz.
40
45
Fl.
1.
p espr.
espr.
ein! Was soll ich hier nun län-ger steh'n? Ich seh' die Mor-gen-
in, why should I lon-ger now stand here? I see the mor-ning-
pp
div.
50

1.
Fl.
Voce
Vl.I
Vl.II
Vla.
Vlc.
Cb.
p
pp
Mit Aufschwung
Con slancio
röt' auf-geh'n, die Mor - gen - röt' zwei hel - le Stern. Bei mei-nem
red ap - pear, the mor - ning - red, two stars so bright, to be with
55
60

1.
Fl.
Voce
Vl.I
Vl.II
Vla.
Vlc.
Cb.
pp
div.
unis.
Schatz da wär' ich gern, bei mei - nem Herz - al - ler - lieb - - -
thee were my de - light, with thee, my heart's best-be - lo - - -
65
70

Wie zu Anfang
Come prima
Fl.
Ob.
Cl.
Tr.
Voce
1.
pp
1. con sord.
p
75
le.
ved.
Das Mädchen stand auf und ließ ihn
The mai-den got up and let him
a 2
sf
ein; sie heißt ihn auch will-kom-men sein.
in, and wel-come, too, she bids to him.
div.
Vl. I
Vl. II
Vla.
80
85

Sehr gehalten
Molto tenuto
Voce
Vl. I
Vl. II
Vla.
Vlc.
Cb.
Will-kom-men lie-ber Knabe mein, so
O wel - come be, now lad-die mine, so
lang hast du ge-stan - den!
long hast thou been stan - ding.
Sie
She
espr.
pp
pizz.
p
90
95
100

reicht ihm auch die schneeweiße Hand.
gives him, too, her snow-white hand,

Von
a-

105   110

 fer - ne   sang die   Nach - ti -   gall; das   Mäd - chen   fing   zu   wei -
far off   sang the   nigh - tin -   gale, the   mai - den   now   to   weep

115

Fl.
Ob.
Cl.
Cor.
Tr.
Voce
Vl. I
Vl. II
Vla.
Vlc.
con sord.
con sord.
1. con sord.
- - nen an.
be - gan.
120
125
Ob.
Cor.
1. 2. a 2
(sord.) dim.
Voce
Ach wei - ne nicht, du Lieb - ste mein, ach
O weep not love, nor tears be thine, o
Vl. I
Vl. II
Vla.
Vlc.
Cb.
sempre pp
pizz.
div.
arco
130

Fl.
Voce
Vl.I
Vl II
Vla.
Vlc.
Cb.
1.
p
wei - ne nicht, du Lieb - ste mein, aufs Jahr sollst du mein Ei - gen
weep not, love, nor tears be thine, with - in a year thou shalt be
arco
pizz.
135
140
Fl.
Ob.
Cl.
Cor.
Voce
Vl.I
Vl.II
Vla.
Vlc.
Cb.
pp
p espr.
1. solo sord.
sein.
mine.
Mein Ei - gen sollst du werden ge -
Mine own thou shalt a - lone be -
div.
145

wiß, wie's kei - ne sonst auf Er - den ist! O Lieb' auf grü-
come as there on all___ the earth is none, o love, on earth

- ner Er - - - - - den.
is none_____

Ich
Must

zieh in Krieg auf grü-ne Haid', die grü - ne Hai - de,die ist__ so
to the wars where green the mead, where green__ the mead__ far way__ doth

170

weit.
lead!

All-wo dort die schönen Trom-
And there where the shin - ing

pizz.

pizz.

pizz.

175

Ob.
Cor.
Tr.
Voce
Vla.
Vlc.
1.
p
sf
pp
ppp
a 2
pe - - ten bla - sen, da ist mein Haus, mein Haus von grü-nem
trum___ pets are blo - wing, there is_ my house, my house of green sod
Ra-sen.
gro-wing.
180
185
190

Lob des hohen Verstands

In praise of lofty intelligence

Fl.
a2
sf
Cl.
2.
a 2
f
Schalltrichter in die Höhe!
L'apertura in aria!
ff
Fg.
a 2
f
Voce
Keck ardito
Einst-mal in ei-nem tie-fen Tal
Once in a low and love-ly vale
Vl. I
Vla.
Vlc.
pizz.
f
10
Cl.
Voce
Kuk-kuck und Nach-ti-gall tä-ten ein Wett' an-schla-gen. Zu
Cuc-koo and Nigh-tin-gale one with t'oth-er com-pe-ted: Which
15

20
1.
Ob.
Cl.
Fg.
a 2
Cor.
1. 2. a 2
Voce
sin- gen um das Mei-ster-stück,
of the two could bet- ter sing
ge-winn' es Kunst, ge -
did chance all me - rit
Vl. I
Vl. II
Vla.
Vlc.
Cb.
pizz.
20

winn' es Glück! Dank soll er da-von tra - gen!
vict'- ry bring: price would to him be met - ed.

Der Kuk-kuck sprach:,,So dir's ge-fällt, hab ich den Rich-ter wählt,"
The Cuc-koo spake: "An' pleased be thou, I'll choose the judge right now".

40 und tät gleich den E - sel er - nen - nen! „Denn
and straight - way the don - key e - lec - ted, "for

weil er hat zwei Oh - ren groß, Oh - ren groß, Oh - ren groß, so
that he has two amp-le ears, amp-le ears, amp-le ears, he

45

Fg.
a 2
Tr.
Timp.
Voce
kann er hö-ren de-sto bos, und, was recht ist, ken - nen"!
there-fore all the bet-ter hears and right may be ex - pec - ted.
Vl. I
Vl. II
Vla.
Vlc.
50
Cor.
Timp.
Voce
55
Sie flo-gen vor den Rich-ter bald. Wie
Eft - soon be - fore the judge they flew, and

dem die Sa – che ward er-zählt, schuf er, sie soll-ten sin – gen!
when he of the con - test knew he bade them to be - gin it.

Fl.
Ob.
Cl.
Fg.
Cor.
Voce
Vl.I
Vl.II
Vla.
1.
a 2
div.
pizz.
arco
Die Nach - ti - gall sang
The Nigh - tin - gale sang
70
Fl.
Cl.
Fg.
Trgl.
Voce
Vl.I
Vl.II
Vla.
Vlc.
lieb-lich aus!
sweet and clear,
Der E - sel sprach: Du
the don-key spake: "Thy
barsch
ruvido
pizz.
75

80
in Es-Mib
Cl.
in B-Sib
1.
ff
f
a2
Fg.
ff
Tb.
p
Timp.
p
Voce
machst mir's kraus! Du machst mirs kraus! I-ja! I-ja! Ich
note is queer, thy note is queer! Yee-haw, Yee-haw, in-
Vl.I
Vl.II
Vla.
p
arco
Vlc.
pizz.
Cb.
p
80

Fl.
Ob.
Cl.
Fg.
a 2
1.
Voce
kann's in Kopf nicht brin - gen!
to my ear can't bring it."
Der
There-
Vla.
Cb.
arco
div.
85
Fl.
Ob.
Cl.
Fg.
Voce
Kuk-kuck drauf fing an geschwind sein Sang durch Terz und Quart und Quint.
on sang quick - ly the Cuc-koo his thirds and fourth and fifth all through,
Vl. I
Vl. II
Vla.
Vlc.
90

Dem E-sel g'fiels, er sprach nur: Wart! Wart! Wart! Dein
which donkey pleased, he spake but: Wait, wait, wait, my

Ur-teil will ich spre - chen, ja spre - chen.
ver-dict I will ren - der, yea ren - der,

Fl.
Ob.
Fg.
Cor.
Voce
Wohl sun-gen hast du Nach - ti - gall! A-ber Kuk - kuck singst
not ill hast sung thou, Nigh - tin - gale, but thou Cuc - koo singst
Vl. I
Vl. II
Vla.
Vlc. e Cb.
arco
arco
105
Cor.
Tr.
Voce
gut Cho-ral! gut Cho-ral, und hältst den Takt fein in - nen, fein
cho - rals well, cho - rals well, and time keepst in fine man - ner, fine
Vl. I
Vl. II
Vla.
Vlc. e Cb.
110

Cl.
Fg.
Cor.
Trb. e Tb.
Voce
Vl. I
Vl. II
Vla.
Vlc. e Cb.
in Es-Mib
pesante
in - - nen! Das srech' ich nach mein' hoh'n Ver-stand,
man - - ner. So with my lof - ty in - tel - lect,
115
Fl.
Ob.
a 2
hoh'n Verstand, hoh'n Verstand und kost' es gleich ein gan-zes Land, so
in - tel-lect, in - tel-lect, and, cost a land it, I di - rect it

laß ich's dich ge - win - nen, ge - win - nen.
go to thee as win - ner, as win - ner.

Kuk-kuck, Kuk-kuck,
Cuc-koo, *Cuc-koo,*

I - ja!
Yee - haw.